# *Outcry*

poems by **Pat Hickerson**

Red Alice Books 2016

Acknowledgements –
Various forms of some of these poems
have previously appeared in:
*Daughter and Mother,*
*At the Grail Castle Hotel, Dawn and Dirty,*
*Punk Me, Rachel My Torment*

Special thanks to:
Evan Myquest, Annie Menebroker,
Doreen Domb, Lelania Arlene and Cynthia Linville
for sharing their talents.

Cover photo courtesy of Lelania Arlene
Cover design by Red Alice Books
Editor: Cynthia Linville

Red Alice Books
P.O. Box 262, Penn Valley, California 95946
U.S.A.

ISBN: 0-9971780-0-0
ISBN: 978-0-9971780-0-5

Library of Congress Control Number: 2016930421

*For Tim*

# Contents –

Introduction by Bill Gainer

# Introduction

Red Alice Books is an imprint of the not for profit arm of The Legends Foundation. We take on projects we feel are at risk of being overlooked because of limited expectations of financial reward. Our prime purpose is to do good things, with good people, for good people. We are not submission based, and we do not look for projects; somehow they find us. Pat Hickerson's *Outcry* is an example of how things often take a crooked path to our door.

I had seen this manuscript early on. Another publisher had asked me to look at it for possible inclusion in their catalog. It was rough, but I loved it. After falling below the radar for a few years, Cynthia Linville brought it to my attention, explaining it was still available and asking if we at Red Alice Books would be interested in taking a fresh look. Having long been charmed by Pat and her poems, I jumped at the opportunity, with one condition – that Cynthia be the project editor. Using a gentle hand, Cynthia brought us this marvelously sculpted book.

It is with great thanks to the Estate of Pat Hickerson, Pat's grandson – Aaron Hickerson, and especially Cynthia Linville that we are able to once again hold Pat in our hearts. Again, thank you all.

*Bill Gainer*
*Red Alice Books*

# *Outcry*

# STRANGE

troubled girl of 14
I turned to Mother
she pulled out a knife
stabbed my shadow

I packed up my dream bag
departed for unknown destinations
heard strange voices
listened to strange music
talked to strange people
loved strange men
wrote strange stories

nothing but strange would do

it was you, Mother,
who sent me soaring
thru the twilight sky of girlhood
into the midnight blue of strange

# RAPTURE

they lived in the west Bronx
used to be called Bronk's Landing
after an old Dutch farmer
bordered the Hudson at Kingsbridge
Peg was a downtown secretary
Andy a teller at Guaranty Trust

we took the IRT uptown to 224th Street
it was Elevated up there
brand-new brick buildings stretched upward
we rushed along the uphill sidewalks

Peg had a half day work that Saturday
came home cleaned the apartment
parquet floors and French doors at the foyer
white porcelain bathroom
a decanter of blue bath salts
Andy made drinks
Peg passed out, fell into bed
Andy found her in the bedroom
bawled her out ... *we've got guests!*
Peg cried
we sat around in the living room, waited
when she recovered she played the baby grand
Pale Hands I Loved Beside the Shalimar
*where are you now? who lies beneath your spell?*
Andy pulled her from the.bench, kissed her

I was a kid
I sat on their bedroom floor
I smelled Peg's Shalimar perfume
I made up stories around their artifacts
a small teakettle gone green on a hob
a table-top tree with crystal leaves

beyond their windows
a maze of other walls and windows
I heard the El train squeal and wheeze
jolt to a stop
move slow again
groan and grunt
Peg's laugh rippled high
pale hands of poetry played the piano again

# BRIGHT STAR

*(sotto voce from the kitchen)*
*what's the matter?*
*hush, it's the boy*
*oh, she ...*

pounds the stairs to her room
to the boy in her mind
the boy with the basketball
the boy who wins
the boy with the freckles
the boy with the soft smile
pale cheeks and giant hands
lie on the couch
wrapped together
his legs encase her, trap her

*what's the matter?*
*it's the boy*

she stalks the carpet squares
opens, closes the desk drawer
riffles her papers
stares out the window
the late sky, studding stars
Bright Star, would I were steadfast ...
the boy fills her mind

she will encase the boy in a poem
wrap his body in words
the boy, she will trap him in her mind
hostage to her senses
she will be steadfast for years to come

*what's she doin' up there?*
*hush, it's the boy*

# INTEMPERANCE

girl and her books
leave campus for home
6 pm she
stands in a lava flow
pulsing magma
from the beat of the dance studio

southbound headlights
pick through Westside winter gloom
shadow the frozen bricks
of Academe

north winds
sink her from sidewalk to subway –
in the train's hot rush and sway
fevered dreams erupt:
last summer's molten kiss consumes her

not the ice-blue embrace
of Mother's house
in the temperate zone

# COMIC BOOK SCENARIO

hey you!  Dracula man!
you still come to me at midnight,
haunt my dreams – my old mentor
tormenting me with advice
sucking the blood from my brain
whipping me to write like a maniac
driving me to revise revise revise
we used to stalk the college corridor together
smoke your Kools in conference

then I propositioned you
drove miles through storm and rain
getting to you
*let's go for a drink* I said
you said *no*
(wrapping your cloak of sublime chastity
about your bony shoulders)
*I'm not like those other professors*
*I don't cheat on my wife!*
subsequently …
you flapped your batwings
flew off to a teaching job
in the Middle East
never to be sighted again
and all this time
your specter has had me by the throat
Dracula man, writer of novels
tall and spare and dark

question:
whyja hafta go an' kill yerself?
(I just found out)
I often wondered where you were
what you were doing
*not writing any more?*

now I learn you've been dead for years
not fair, Drac!
to go without letting me suck *you* dry

# JOANNA AT THE SUBWAY

on a midtown sidewalk
black her skirt, tight her style
boot-heeled and hustling smart
go-get-it! Times Square!
she elbows the reaming mass
gumspots paste cement
step on a crack, break your mother's back
downtown stop, dank step takedown
grab the green banister
sling the tote, watch the pockets
read the signs
crowding speechless
make the change
pump the turnstile
jar the metal
dizzy the whirl
here it comes
retreat from the edge, squeal of wheels
press forward, cross the gap
through the closing doors, shut in
grasp the pole, hang on for the lurch
ride she goes – 34th Street
and sway…

# REVLON CALL FOR LOVE

pink angora sweater fuzzy soft
tight along her breasts
walks down Main Street
past vacant storefronts
pink as a baby cloud floating
lipstick Revlon purple pink
tiny toes like bald rodents
wriggling bare Super Lustrous
the polished tips Nipple Pink new Siren tricks
Vagina Rose Revlon's deepest shade

she's pink as pink can be
virgin thighs a call for love
swaying across the railroad bridge
*wrap those Lustrous lips around this*, he says
from a dark doorway
save her the best shot
Money Shot
Revlon's most alluring fragrance
more potent than Flair or She or Downtown Girl
turns your spit and semen fuchsia pink

walks down Main Street
hugging herself in the pleasure of it
the looks the whistles the hands
the call to arms
Revlon Punk the new shade
*wrap those Revlon lips around this*
he says motioning her
she could comply
at a doorway
to kneel between his, if she thinks about it
outstretched legs

## ALONG THE SIDEWALK 1942

he followed her –
growled with passion
eyebrows wobbled
nerves tumbled
reached for her, shadow turned fierce

where an arrow struck
his loins collapsed in grief
he fell to the cement
she who had a talent for incitement
could do nothing to stanch the blood
seeping from his wound

## JUST FOR A MINUTE

he said
I want to go inside you
    just for a minute
    just to get the feel of you
and I said yes
so he did
    just to get the feel of me
he said I want to go inside you
    for a minute
to get the feel of you
and I said yes
    and he did
and I said I'm glad you did
and he said I wanted to
    get the feel of you
I said I know

## ACROBATIC

cartwheeling onto your bed
I landed in a split on your navel
a backbend across your abs
and my toes whirled into your groin
a headstand while clutching your thighs
and my tongue arched at your muscle
front-over placed me at your mouth
backflip settled knees against knees ...
ready?

much later a handstand took us apart
somersault brought me to the floor
walkover vaulted me to the door
and out –

# FRANKIE'S FRIED EELS

… in a cab
on her way to Tipitina's for jazz
she thought she saw Frankie Chenier
her once lover
running down Prytania Street…

back there with Frankie
*café au lait* skin sleek black hair
green eyes spatter of freckles
his sudden smile as he gazed at her nipples
*y'all so pink! all pink'n cream!*

she died every night
held captive in Frankie's arms
like the city they lived in
caught between the Mississippi
and Lake Pontchartrain
in the crescent of its moonless joy

she loved the feel of Frankie's lips
firm and full and well-defined
as the streetcar tracks
that run from St. Charles Avenue past the Circle
with its fine statue of Lee, downtown to Canal Street
tracks quietly erect in their low-lying path
along the neutral ground

watched Frankie cook, watched live eels dance
amid his long brown fingers
he sliced them in thirds as they squealed in agony
mangled them in butter with bits of scallion
some flour thrown in, wine, cognac
swamped them in mustard sauce….

# AUGUST, HER WAR, 1944

holding close to her breast
mean-patched jowls of the city
lush stink of sidewalk
hard as August cement
rusty as chrome fenders
humidity bears down
imminent as a double-decker bus
pounding Fifth Avenue
in heavy weather

office doorknobs
clang of monitor bells
clacking typewriter keys
wounded women sturdy as desks
bandaged in black
their men at Anzio
howl *Dirty Gertie from Bizerte*
in mud-crusted heat and sweat

sixteen summers and now her war
whirling white her free-swing skirt
the time of high heels
thigh-gartered nylons
holding her sailor's hand
his jumper cast to the far Pacific
Leyte and New Caledonia
1944 his bell bottom letters
dark ribbons of hope
twine her heart

smoke and litter
hot winds
swell from the W. 23$^{rd}$ Street subway stop –
the train grinds, squeals
halts in deadly dust

# COLD IN KILBURN

and where were you?
off at a London racetrack
throwing our cash at losers

it was cold up in that dark room
on Kilburn Road
away from light and life
rented cheaply to tourists
by indifferent hosts

what was I doing there anyway
when I could have been dancing my heart out
at Roseland
or listening to geniuses on $52^{nd}$ Street
colleagues of Dizzy and Miles
with bigger and louder horns than yours
cuddled closely in hot New York clubs?

but no, here I was
a storm coming, lightning streaked the window
waiting for you in the dark and cold
wondering at my choice

## HEIGHT

you said, I'm not very tall
I said, but you have a hard body
I once loved a man who was shorter than you
I loved him more than anything
you said, did he have a hard body
I said, not as hard as yours

you bent and kissed my cheek

soon we lay in the woods
I rested my head on your chest
your feet reached beyond mine
see, I said, you're much longer than I am
you said the trees are taller than both of us
I said your arms are long, too
like branches of your body
how easily they wrap around me
you said, your body is softer than mine

I reached up and kissed you on the lips

soon your hard body
was stretched over my soft body
your lips at my lips
your legs stretched longer than mine
we lay still for awhile
leaves rustled above
sun went down, stars came out
moon came up
you moved within me
I said, I love you more than anything

## MY CRICKET

nerve and sinew
boy of my bones
coming out on the New York side
cold December day
dark density of a world city
few crickets chirping here
only you, my poet boy
held high before me
our blood smeared your hard head
sign of great passion to come
as you slipped silently
in and out my door
and back again

I drink in your eyes
your world
your sweet soul
your cricket cry of wisdom
echoes in my ears

## LIKE AN IDIOT

I followed him to Boston on the train
although he didn't know it at the time
I saw him kiss a woman in the rain
I understood the reason and the rhyme

although he didn't know it at the time
I'd feared another woman in his heart
I understood the reason and the rhyme
I guess our love was doomed right from the start

I'd feared another woman in his heart
someone he'd known from many years ago
I guess our love was doomed right from the start
I wept to see their kiss was long and slow

someone he'd known from many years ago
Would now the mistress of his thoughts remain
I wept to see their kiss was long and slow
I followed him to Boston on the train

## MURDER ON PARK AVENUE

is she sad?
hell, no
she's as sparkly as springtime out here
whatever else is going on...
she's got it all in hand
spike heeled boots and a rhinestone shirt
she just dumped her sweetie
or was it the other way 'round?
funny how her brain is a blank
all she remembers is that day he got so mad at her
he tried to throw her from his tenth floor window...

whatever ... she's hard as cinders
hard as the mascara on her lashes
the Revlon nails at her fingertips
stalking past chrome and concrete
she won't let it disturb her days
she can take him or leave him
she doesn't care –
let him ball that back-door slut ...

cars and chrome and concrete
glass walls and green lights
mascara and miniskirts
nails and tails: she'll be wanton at the Waldorf
he never really loved her, did he?

brass gleaming all around
brass banisters, brass lanterns
Grand Central Station glitters
diamond of the city
she'll buy a real diamond some day
she'll be diamond-hard
hard enough to scratch a glass window
hard enough to drop-kick that old guy
limping across the street against traffic
she'd love to see him or someone else she knows
gut-squashed in the fast lane ...

## DAWN AND DIRTY

sunrise
here I am filthy
from the worm holes
that housed me during the night
we hold our breath
in the tunnel of your bed
lip to lip
limb to limb
as she knocks I am forbidden to breathe
or make a sound
she keeps knocking, calling out

slipshod through crackling subways
breast exposed to the roil of the strap hanging crowd
your hand at my mouth
your body suffocating mine
while he thrashes her under and over
unwieldy wooden turnstiles
ironworks where squealing wheels
jut in and out of grout-grained stations
always seeking a home
she looks to you for comfort
poor baby she's been laid up for weeks
beaten silly by her movie star husband
lying drunk on the rat tracks with his new mistress

she keeps knocking
whining and squalling like wind
blown into the grime of early light
my earrings that I left on the tiles
never saw them again after that night
when I held my breath as a favor to you
which girlfriend did you give them to?

not that I cared
groping around down here
slow climb to the El
rusted rails to morning

# RED HOT

it was still morning
and he began to burn
in a room of many windows
looking out on a side street of the city

watched her with those shoes
she was barefoot in jeans
and a flowered pajama top
flowers red as a cat's tongue
as though she had just hopped out of bed
husband a minus since dawn
they were gold spike-heeled sandals
she held them in her lap
played with the straps
as she might play with any man
her hands small, fingers tender soft

in the room a brown leather couch
an upright piano, stool to whirl
a TV set on a bench
a chair upholstered green
where he chose to sit
after she answered the door
and invited him in

she took in his rap
from a deeper chair
where she nestled careless
her scorched honey hair kicking back
across the cushion
turned toward him, gave him the once-over
he began to burn

it would happen that night
they would meet on a corner
the flowers on her pajama top still red
red as a cat's tongue, that's what she was
a kitten he could throw high in the air
catch in his arms when she fell
and he would explore her
find her parts as hot as a killer's tongue
pulsing blood-red as last night's sunset

## DESPERADOES

on the sidewalk
outside the pickup bar
she whirled around
her silk skirt ballooning
like a wind puffed umbrella
Young Dino
sleek and tough
 Said *you're so hot*
(and she bought it)

they were driving through
Golden Gate Park
in his banged up Chevy
Dino showed her his gun
packed neatly into a shoulder holster
the deserted meadows
even the trees were lonely
their bleakness spread
across the curving roads

she said *I thought you were going*
*to take me to a party in Oakland*
*I want to dance*

he laughed *we'll dance at my place*
she thought of his gun
its intricate killing design
nestled close to his heart

*his* place:
an underground cave
the shower in the one room
the toilet out back somewhere
he claimed his *real* place
was being redecorated
(she bought that, too)
he opened his leather jacket
there it was
a loaded midnight tool

as she pleasured him
she wondered

did he ever pull it out and say
*this is a stickup?*
she giggled and flung away
making an earthquake in the bed
what was high went low
what was hard went soft
Dino glared – *Hey! Watchit!*

the following week
she was back home in L.A.
Dino called at 3 in the morning
waking her teenaged sons
her husband rolled over, grunted
*it's probably for you*
she tossed out of bed bleary …
Dino needed serious money
she said she could send
a twenty

he hung right up
she whispered to the hushed household
*he thought I was rich …*

## PORN STAR

Candi Cone – where
did you ever get that name?
just because you were baptized Candace?
pretty little girl of the Bronx
dancing and dreaming
like any other good little girl
daddy, a jazz musician
mommy left early on
a cruel stepmother
(or maybe only frightened)
what you saw in your bedroom at night
daddy and your older sister
swallow the shame ... still

it helped you make it to the big time
heroin and coke made it easy, too
so did the Mitchell Brothers
famous in San Francisco
*and* New York
in cafés, men stop and stare at you
they've seen you in their best dreams
and on film
the forbidden kind

now you're sleek and sixty
directing, producing
nice porn films for the ladies
to educate them, Candi Cone

## THE ARGENTINE FISHERMAN

she leans against him
The Master's big belly
wraps her stiletto heels
around his chunky calves
she's his pupil, his darling fish
allowed to lean against him
tease him with scarlet lips
sleek sheath scaled with silver sequins
flutter of mascara
black patent leather
stocking and garter
she slips his way
dip and sway
he pitches his rod to a tango stream
the alley to the pampas
through violin, bandoneón, piano ripple
against the rhythm into parrot jungle
palmetto gaze
lash of silver monkey tail
dense as the Rio Plato
drains back to city stink and tremor
hum of boot and bellow
The Master's life, not hers
she leans dead against him
his master rod has caught
a fish
leaping silver from the river

## WHILE SHE WAITS

her river
broad and rhythmically lapping
tuned to a deliberate surge
carries her long unhurried story on its back
totes her cargo season to season
washes the banks of the city
where she was born Sunday morning
first saw daylight
three blocks from waterside

while she waits

her river nods to the Palisades
shallow waves sun-sparkled
holds up bridges shore-to-shore
burrows tunnels through its trenches
ferries one way and another
barges up and down
steams between Battery Park and the Liberty statue
powers into the Atlantic

that's her ocean
(waiting)
where soon she will float on her back
stare up at the stars
it will be Sunday night by then

# ROMANCE

*rape, I want you to get the feel of it,*
said the Green-Eyed Knight to his lady-in-arms
and she obeyed at 3 AM
bedded down at Grail Castle Hotel
once the inn of gold-seekers
storied of old, waters edge
Port Camelot

he held her
rammed against the bedstead's iron bars
head twisted round
hustled into her
deep, wide
too deep, too wide –

hers was a small space skin space
soft place
linked to rose petals and nerve tendrils
trickled down the backs of her legs
locked in currents of pain
the rest of her life …

in too deep
was it only a 3-second nap
from all the fire pumped into her? or
from passion perverted
its saturnine face darkly smiling
into hers?

she-who-must-be-punished
– she began to wonder
floated a cautionary sailboat
out across Reason's lake

## ABYSS

the hole kept getting bigger

she staggered out of her bedroom
down the hall to the dining room
and there, by one of the chairs
she was stopped by the sight of the hole
spreading from where she stood
she was about to fall into it

she didn't care about her husband, only
her children
(who knew nothing about
the nightmare man at her heels)
though she could no longer see her children while
standing over their bodies in bed

to the hospital for pills
*have you been assaulted?*
*no ... yes ... I wanted it*

she trembled –
Mother was reading *Bluebeard*
wives hung on hooks in the locked closet
blood pooled at their dangled feet
Mother's thready voice called up to the lookout tower:
*Sister Anne, Sister Anne, do you see my brothers coming?*

the pills kicked in
she fell asleep hiding the telltale key
(Fatima waiting for rescue)

pills
hypo
breathless she slid down a no-holds brick wall
the abyss waited below

she pretended to be alive
ghost in a foreign land

# HIGH TIMES ON FILLMORE STREET 1968

poor Bobby had a bullet in his thigh
he wouldn't tell me who had put it there
we lit up joints to reach a mellow high
then danced till dawn and scarcely had a care

he wouldn't tell me who had put it there
his girlfriend's flat was soon filled up with folks
we danced till dawn and scarcely had a care
we never had a shortage of shared tokes

his girlfriend's flat was soon filled up with folks
I hoped this night would never have an end
we never had a shortage of shared tokes
to leave at dawn would on a cab depend

I hoped this night would never have an end
but Clarence had the money so we left
to leave at dawn would on a cab depend
I mourned for Bobby; and I felt bereft

but Clarence had the money so we left
poor Bobby had a bullet in his thigh
I mourned for Bobby, and I felt bereft
we shared a final joint and said goodbye

# FUNKY SUN

funk rocks me
walking the streets with you
after a rainy day

rain pounds the window
then you show up
funky sun comes out

sun goes down
house goes dark
you come to get me
sun rises

midnight finds me in the dark
watching the street for you
oh there you are
suddenly the funky sun!

some nights black as sin
I meet you at the corner
sun is shining

## ORANGE LIGHT

why does your kiss at sunset
make me howl like a wolf all night long
it must be this strange orange light
I've been prowling the woods ever since
nosing out the smaller animals
crying in their ears
roughing them up and twirling them in the leaves
not really wanting to hurt anyone
but yearning to sink my teeth into your flesh
shake you into my heart for good
never let you go

## NOW LOOK WHAT YOU'VE DONE

you, you
who have set me on fire
like sunlight igniting the color blue
I'm now a passion tree
poems flaming along the branches
I'm all my own color
red hot
a new ignition of words
holding the lit match to the tree
you the ignition

## TANGO MASTER

her patent leather heel spikes his ankle
the portly man in black suit and white shirt
jerks her thru the alley

a silk scarf covers his wattles
aging fat man lithe as a snake
desire still potent

she takes it
she takes it all
the press of his hand on her back
the turn of his lofty thigh
the grip on her gut

she takes the hard pull
it rips her apart
*brava* the torn dress
the mad tongue
the dark heart
pushes her to the stony plaza
to the rise and fall of accordions
the soaring street singers
to the circle of gasping onlookers
they cheer her pliant swoon
dazed eyes

## MEMORY OF MY DANCER

pressed tight against your orchid
sienna in your skin
glint of tango in your eye
Argentina on your tongue
gleam of moonlight on your brow
other dancers pushed us closer
barely moving
dizzy in your heated hills
we climbed the peak
shaking underground
my earthquake house
slanting floor
open door

## TRIANGLE

ping!
a tinny sound to it
little kids play at music
as you have played with me
while she looked on …

say, weren't you the one?
grabbed me by the tit
hurled me into the air
caught me on your pointed boot
whirled me around
hugged me tight
forced my lips into your needy neck

while she looked on …

your tail between your legs
sniffed me out
snuggled into my armpit
leered at my breast (but slyly)
kept up the front
while she looked on
mocked your puritan soul

your three-cornered hat
thrown down in the grass
mad matador faces an addled cow
out to pasture feeding slowly
ruminates on her milky past
rethinks her lineup of well-hung bulls

the pasture now *your* stadium
your wife the jeering crowd
I fall back, tired of
waiting for the prick of your lance
hear her triumphant *ho ho*
from the nearby stands

let me tell you something, sonny
I never really wanted you – anyway

# BABS OF NEW ORLEANS 1965

it's Saturday evening again
along the steaming crescent
*where ya goin', sugar?* out, out, out
front door slams

Babs stands in the parking lot
Eddie Price's pool hall on Magazine Street –
smokin' hot 9<sup>th</sup> grade bitch queen
long legs seven league boots
thigh skirt tight, shining hair
falls back between the angel wings
greets a striving boy-child
pool cue twists his fingers
his smirking mask bobs at her breast
he offers up a Marlboro butt
from his baby lips to her Revlon lips

Babs strides down Prytania Street
high school boys drive by
chanting obscene
she laughs, offers them the finger
escapes into Taffy's house
with Jay and Rachel and Rick
friends from Fortier
smoke and drink
listen to the Beatles, dance from room to room
sing hello to Sunday morning
Babs hasn't given herself up yet; she's picky
she wants McCartney –

headfirst out thru Taffy's window
mom's *sugar* going home from the long night
she dreams along rat-alleys, past shotgun squalor
shell-strewn levees
in shadow and rising sun
the lowering city river-shaped

## ANOMIE HOTEL ON THE RIVER

I could have jumped from here
river in my eyes
down I'd go
river in my eyes
down to the street
river in my eyes
14$^{th}$ floor cheap hotel
river in my eyes
Palisades yonder
but river in my eyes
high as high could have jumped
summer sidewalk
sweating terror
far from home
hit cement
river in my eyes
only one roach
river in my eyes
peek from drawer
brown antennae gone too far
searching for surprise
river in my eyes
I could have jumped
river in my eyes
share the shower, man next door
couple fighting down the hall
river in my eyes
where's my home?
river in my eyes

## OUR SHEETS ARE COOL AND SMOOTH

daylight opens our bed
your voice like driveway gravel
stir of chimes in the wind
guttering leaves
squirrel-patter on the roof
early rain on hot pavement
I can smell it, taste it
your breath sweet as oranges
your arm at my neck
your arm hair tickles
your fingers burrow
my fingers play your tongue
your tongue not so rough as a cat's
your skin the color of teak
my lips on your skin

our sheets are cool and smooth
pillow deep and down
sink in
your body my wall against the day

## SUMMER NIGHT SWIM

in the stone quarry flooded
you and I hot as July
shallow the moon glitter
toes paled, lips silvered
metallic glaze on a gushing plain
voices a net of echoes
ears silenced we leave the others
sink through the midnight pool
rocky nip of boulders
fevered jut of flesh
how we grow under the press of fingers
caress of dreams in a bowl of water
cool
lapping at arms and legs
your arms and legs
wrapping me at the flood

# SEA CHAIN

riotous waters
my lifelong quarry
hollowed from stone age monuments
chipped from ice-tormented streams
flooded, receded
kin to Caspian, Azov

wading in, toes scratched
by mollusk shells
knees rimmed by algae
eyelids fluttered by triplefin

beneath its dark mask
the deluge seethes brilliant
emerald-charged
blood-crust mammoth-jaws leer

from Varna to Samsun
from Sukhumi to Constanta
hand over hand back and forth
the stunning swim

my dream-inflated head
bobs above rowdy waves
I float kick thrust
shun the airless floor
*anaerobia* waiting to dissolve
what falls bottomward

the Black Sea then my pool
nourished by bold torrents
from the Caucasus
rushing into the basin
once a brackish lake acid-faced

I, too –

change the plunging course
force a hole through the Bosporus
the Dardanelles
tumble into the strait-laced Aegean
greet the Mediterranean ...

# BACK STORY

last night her mind reeled with words
about the Gulf of Finland
under the midnight sun
the two little naked boys she'd once seen
running through warm surf
on the Karelian Peninsula

> *someone told her his father dunked him*
> *in Lake Algonquin for a bath, he was only 3*

in her sleep
she named the little boys
Chickie and Viktor
over and over
Chickie and Viktor

> *she saw his little white body*
> *lowered in and out, sudsed*
> *ordered to hold his breath –*
> *he gasped, rigid with fright*
> *ducked a second time to rinse*

that summer in Russia
she'd gone with fellow travelers
to a nearby café
danced the crowded floor
the bandleader sang *densink chick to chick*
a Fred Astaire song
excited at entertaining the Americans
Chickie and Viktor weren't there
they were too young

> *too young too terrified*
> *to be lowered into the icy lake*

but the little boys kept running naked
through her dream
little white bodies
in and out of gentle sunlit surf
at the Gulf of Finland
Chickie and Viktor
again and again

# TOUCH OF SAND

we lie here
white-hot sand
ocean rumbling beyond
dig our toes into pure heat
sun hypnotic, demanding
your lips are alive
cool to the touch
you suck my fingers into density
first one finger, then the other
I press my open mouth against yours
seek your tongue
a sandy vein that gives surprise

sand in our hair
sand on our lips
rivulets tucked in the corners
we murmur, grains fall away
sand in our ears make an echo

touch of sand for a glistening day

give me your lips I'll surprise them
touch my sandy lips
and touch again
take me by the lips
the lips, the tongue, the vein inside

## MOSCOW APPLEJACK 1973

bought me some ruble-cheap
bottlejack applejack
bitters and brandy
jacked for an age
dark stuff strong stuff
murky brown bottle
should have stuck with vodka, stupid!

lying here in a cloudy cabin
on the outer grounds of
the Intourist Hotel
on Moscow's broad boulevard

and all I can see
weeds
chain link fence
not even the Kremlin fortress riverside
tho yesterday I saw Lenin's body
alive and well under glass

bloody Aussie kids
partying all night in their tents
(nobody stopped the racket)
now at last they're asleep
I thought this country was strict!

quiet under a dimmed-out sun
hangover cabin my place
happy cramped up

I'd rather be stupid but safe here
on well-guarded "Russky" Street
than Stateside stupefied by
the daily celebration of catastrophe

Russia smells different
sniff the enigma

## SOFIA DARLING

all the way down from Prague
sleeping 22 hours upright by train
from a throbbing jet lag week
to you, darling, your soothing yellow walls
puff-cobbled streets
hotel staircase swathed in red carpet
we descended like royalty from our
lace curtained room

spawned ourselves out
to your sun-plenished square, darling
under our café table
dark and dusty gypsy kids
crouched grinning
waited for leftovers

a *Courvoisier* at the bar
then the restaurant
*shopska* salad
old flap-foot waiter
seven years an elevator operator in Chicago
came all the way back to you, darling
slow-pitched Slavic Sofia –
he couldn't stay away

## OVERNIGHT IN HERO CITY 1979

now to Smolensk
arrived by train from Moscow
at the "camping" woods
summertime trees
drooped over our heads
broken-down cottages
attached like aging friends
about to die
in a surround of moss and mold

could I sleep in this?

powerful enemy the mold
waged flaming war
in the sinus cavity
all night my dreams of fire-power
I a citizen-soldier of Smolensk
fighting the Germans 1941
I take a stand, shot down
stand up, shot down
stand ... my city smolders
burnt-out nubs
smoking sinuses –

in the morning
a plate of yogurt covered in coarse sugar
pure snow under ice crystals
not the same old caviar
we'd had at the other camps
our teeth popping
golden baby beads piled on
infant rounds of bread

so it was yogurt and sugar
and back to the train station
then on to Minsk
in a straight line west

## VARNA

at Pobiti Kamani
ancient site of oracles
she doesn't remember a
dry plain of underwater stones
only a sway of delicate birch trees
forested in the yellow sand of Black Sea soil

becalmed among the dappled spirits
she heard them sigh
in the language of Bulgaria
she was quieted anyway

## LAST TIME I SAW MOSCOW

don't know what it's like now
from 40 years ago
still drunks sprawled along Nevsky Prospekt?
cops throwing them into paddy wagons?
midnight New Years Eve
toasting with vodka the everyday drink
red velvet hotel's long tables crowded
next morning what a layout of breakfast
hot cereal, eggs, sausage, golden caviar
for lunch borscht in a workers' restaurant
later sitting in a crowded café
across the table from an elderly WWII soldier
honor medal on his lapel dark-eyed blonde at his side
Beatles music, dancing
hot with vodka and loud voices
stamping of feet on Red Square bricks
St. Basil's cathedral onions
cater-cornered to the Kremlin
Lenin finally serene in his glass coffin
guards at the ready
yanked my hand out of my pocket
cold air and snow
babushkas sweeping the streets
their raggedy straw brooms

## XMAS FOG

here I am
like a tramp steamer mist-bound
out in the middle of the Pacific
peering eastward through density
to the Golden Gate Bridge and the city beyond
to you, darling boy
sequestered in rehab on Harrison Street
bereft of your beloved bottles
(vodka, gin, J&B)
waiting for the fog to lift

I wish you luck, Son
now 50
you were the luxury liner
once speeding through sparkling currents
you were supposed to take the world by storm
with your sleek gifts of body and spirit

now I, the old mother tramp
I call out to you in my foghorn voice
as I cradle a mug of warm milk

*Happy Holidays!*

## BLEARY MORNING

when the eyes are hardly open
I moon over you
as though you were still alive
sun on a sunless day

you were born at dawn
bleary January day
shadowed by a great cathedral
God announced your birth
in the voice of a surly head nurse
she threw you down on the bed
tried to alert you to the world
open your eyes she said
you were her favorite –

little golden baby
didn't wake up for 6 months
finally rolled over, hit the floor
cried out

my poor darling
hurting all your life
sometimes the sun came out
radiant but harsh
60 years later a nurse with a needle
put you to sleep

## AT NIGHTFALL

the dream place
in bed
under a cool sheet
and downy blanket
pale green memories
those you love
become poems
words cool and settle
reach for the pen
the paper the joys
like kisses in your palm
you blow to the window
where mother moon peers in
to tuck you safe
the smiling coin
through chinks in the blind
dazzle of the big silver face
treasure
at the start of night

# WHAT I SAW FROM MY HOTEL WINDOW
## ON MY 80th BIRTHDAY

an expanse of still water running deep, slow, hardly moving
(like me now)
and hidden in its depths – outrageous, secret, tumbling life
as in the note I wrote 45 years ago
I said to him I am sitting, an exile from our love,
at a window on 48th Avenue
looking out at the Pacific
next stop – China
wishing myself a world away
from the pain of having to give you up
years later, you, now a dead man
buried faraway in Alabama
you are feeling no pain
and I feel almost none

# WE RETURN TO THAT STREET

under my breath
in a corner of my odd-angled heart
again we leave the ghost place on W. 7th Street
we walk out to the fringe of the city
much of the long night
still left to us
the cracked sidewalks
the weedy glass-littered lots
arm in arm
your wasted bone scrapes my withered flesh
we sit at the hamburger counter, remember –
how our bellies were once hot with hunger?

then back to the Pack Train Hotel
up the broad wooden staircase
its hollowed steps heave and squawk
under our clanked feet

you stand in the doorway
your sharp-jointed finger at your disappeared lips
*shhhh …*
before we turn into the $2 room-for-a-night
to resume our sacred rituals:
dry lick
dead stick

# NUMBERS

do you think I care
about your numbers?
I rejoice in your lovers
the many you've had
the many to come
to run out of fingers
for counting
or toes
you belong to the world
and the world is yours
so count your way to heaven
consider yourself blessed

## ROCK ME

skyscraper daddy I call you
my hyperbolic New York pal
built on the phallic principle
stable as bedrock
winsome as the Waldorf
rock and rush
rock me, daddy
let me hug you
I'm a building-hugger
tall as a tree
thick as Grant's Tomb
brutish as the Brooklyn Bridge
squeeze me, won't you?
your hair slick as tar
lips wet as rainy streets
ply me at the Plaza
your stump strains …
stand up for me
no falling down
like the Twins, those wimps!
swing me onto your saddle
slip me into your subway
liberate me at the Library
tail me in your taxi
hump me in the Hudson
crazy gone as the Astor Bar
juggle me daddy
diddle me silly
under your lunatic lamppost
down Fifth, up Madison
boost me at the ballet
frisk me at the Fraunces
cradle me at Columbia
ball me in Bryant Park
beat me daddy, eight to the bar

# LYING HERE WITH YOU, DON

murmuring couples lie around us in the dark
nowhere else to go
except to the grassy midnight lawns of Central Park
our fever is enhanced
hearing the echo of embrace
on the green grass of Central Park
while the rest of the city towers above
concrete steeples in the near distance
office-lit windows peer down
Central Park West and South
the north end ancient with brownstone
a cathedral forever building
and we are quiet in our cocoon
with others beside us
quiet and murmuring glide
let it flow
one couple unaware of the other
except to hear the endless soft murmuring
like fleshy insects invading the grass
spill seed and sperm in a quiet way
not to bother anyone
nowhere else to go—
the midnight silent lawns of Central Park

# PURSUIT ON W. 115<sup>TH</sup> STREET

it was wasn't the first time
you lay down for me, Don
nor the last

*your strange torpor*

in that corner room of yours
we sometimes practiced sorcery for hours
    (eye of moon
      moon of mercury)

drawn shade
baked yellow by sun
throbbing light
heated the room to hyperbole
music was there
    (you beat the tambourine
    I blew the penny whistle)
terror and pain too

no matter how many times
I knocked on your door
no matter how many times
you let me in—
well…

*you danced with men? was that it?*

that building on 115<sup>th</sup> Street
was demolished years ago
you died an old man, Don
somewhere else

## BEFORE YOUR DEATH I DREAMED

we climbed the stairs of an office building
climbing high up
walking the empty corridors
roaming the empty rooms
we walked and walked
exploring
asking each other questions
arguing
climbing higher and higher
until you reached the pinnacle
look, you said, I'm at the top
you leaned out the window
I can see Woman's Hospital
(where we were born, 22 years apart)
oh no, I said, they tore down Woman's Hospital years ago
no, I see it, it's still there at 109th and Amsterdam
it can't be
but I see it, wait I'll check it out online
you looked around the empty room for a computer

now you were leaning far out over the windowsill
waving to the crowds on the street below
you turned to me *I'm at the top*
*I made it all by myself*

yes you did, I said

## VIGIL

when I wake
to the warning moan …
the 3 a.m. train you loved
I dream you are no longer
boxed ashes in a closet
but an impatient spirit
hurried eastward
across singing rails
to the New York sunrise
where you were born

## SHAPE OF FRED HAINES (1936-2008)

tales of your pale-haired groin
lit up a thousand smoky flights

*Ulysses* man 1967
you put Joyce onscreen
you an Oscar boy – I could well believe it

and all the time
at home between your Gypsy lips
a Gitane

I knew you before the Gitanes
you and your leather jacket in Berkeley
KPFA up the stairs downtown
broadcast Lenny Bruce at midnight
almost lost our license
yours and Dede's flat on Wheeler Street
(walls painted black)
chess at the Steppenwolf
staff party at Gert's
my Friday night blowout
you at the piano
black shades hid your fire blue eyes
dazzled by connection

I dreamed of trips-out in the dark
as if my earthy Fred-shaped path
could fit your jigsaw map
your traveled thighs outdistanced mine –

you left town
then I left town
my alternate route as crazed as yours

Gitanes finally got you
Venice on the Pacific
solitary cottage
lungs blackened

## THE HAUNTING

this isn't a TV show
where teams of ghost hunters
wield their technological toys
inspect old houses
hear whimpers and whispers
the restless dead
orbs appear
spooks shoot across space
(or are they just vagrant balls of camera light?)

this is a real haunting
a man you'd like to forget
somehow he doesn't go away
always there inside you
gnawing at your innards
a savage process that will wound you

## WEB

at sunset
she found herself
caught in a whirl of white
gauzy strands
ghosts of yesterday
cobwebs
closing in on her
she held her breath

the web danced around her
not to be taken seriously
the sun started down
in flight from day
she remembered a strong figure
standing immovable before her
she spoke to him
found him elusive
till he made a strange declaration
about herself
and him

it was the poetry of sun going down
red flares pierced a drift of clouds
she floated
without pitch or mold
hands over eyes
not to see what had happened
waiting for his hand held out
sick with wanting

# FUMBLE NIGHT

darkness shelters her fetish
she pities the old man
trembling voice
bubbling eyes
fumbling fingers
scratchy beard
wispy hair
leather skin

he dreams
orchids tossed to the moon
bubbles in the flute
the champagne of her eyes

he must lie by the pool
legs too weak to swim
he will await her
she will come to him dimly
through an opening of dim desire
out of the water dimly seen
dimly felt
hands reach for her
he senses she is young
a rose petal
to press and stroke
he reaches, he fumbles

she lies down beside him in the dark
smooths his hair
*watch the water*, she tells him,
*see how it laps the moonlight*
*silver-crested like your hair*
his bedtime story
while she strokes him dimly
dimly felt
dimly seen
she grasps his water-worn cock
it quivers dimly
dimly seen
dimly felt

## NAKED

filled with his eyes
her hot secret burning her
knew his eyes
filled with them
saw everything
he was all eyes
she saw it all
caught by surprise
his secret look
her eyes
her secret

## THE DEAD MAN NOVEL

chapter one
you, once so darkly alive
now 20 years dead in your Alabama grave
beyond pain and joy

chapter two
we rode down 80
to a hotel on West 7th Street
up the broad wooden staircase
to a simple room
bed, pine-sol bucket, and bare bulb hanging
memorized the ceiling cracks
geography of my soul

chapter three
I waited on a park bench
you promised to meet me there
you never came

# EXPLANATION FOR THE MAN
## STILL WAITING AT THE CORNER

on a decayed place I stumbled
(a street turned savage through hard times ...
shots heard in the distance)
finding *you* there with a chalice of burning liquid
thirsty I drank your dark face
long nights at the Grail ensued
    (she became someone else
    designs of the cracked ceiling her new map of the world
         billboard astride the Port of Oakland
         flashed the Year of Our Lord 1962 ...
    on her back, aflame under his ministrations
    and the walls echoed *baby baby baby*
    swarm of alien bees engorged her soul)
you spoke of your life
I reveled in its martyrdom
desperate master
I pleaded for more
to give myself up to your crucified city
melt my bones into its spiked streets
forsake my own life to live out more of yours
that spiraled across me –

    and

    (when the last bell tolled
    she knew she couldn't
    follow him)

    down

# CAN'T STAND THE RAIN

the rain, she says
can't stand the rain
as she sprints thru the park
slips down to the subway
rides across town
elbows through crowds
dodges the rain
enters Bloomingdale's
riffles through racks
runs out to Lex
buys the *Times*
reads the weather report
can't stand the rain
reaches her apartment
heats up coffee
hugs her dogs
sprawls on the couch
shuffles cards
plays the Ace
snubs the Queen
honors the King
screws the Jack
looks thru the window
admires the rain
from a distance

## YOUR HEAT

I'm cold and
your heat rocks me
you dear old fox
you've wounded me
where I longed to be
wounded
your big belly
my cushion against despair
your white beard
my notion of Santa Claus
grown kind and loving
not a scary thing
your hands hold mine
your lips close in on mine
your eyes cuddle me
stay with me
stay
with me

## WAITING FOR YOUR KISS

here I am
my pillow soft
the moon high and hot
it lights the open window
whitens my sheets
outlines my lips
I'm waiting for you
and your good-night kiss

## CRY

ready for anything
come get me
I don't care if you have to come from Mars
bring your car here
I hear you drive like a maniac
just what I want the mood I'm in
screech your tires pull up in the parking lot
jump out of the car
run upstairs to my place
you say *what's wrong, kid?*
I say *none of your business*
*just get me outta here*
we'll ride and ride
all over the valley
up and down
take me to a casino
give me quarters I'll play the slots
booze me punk me with drugs
open me up diddle me silly
shove it in
let it have its own ride
in and out
don't wake me at the end
let me sleep
sleep
sleep

**Patricia Hickerson,** a graduate from Barnard College, is a former Warner Bros. dancer, copy editor, and *Penthouse* fiction writer. Hickerson has published the chapbooks, *Rachel My Torment* and *Dawn and Dirty*, and the book, *Punk Me*. Her work has appeared in numerous journals and broadsides, including: *At Grail Castle Hotel*, *Convergence*, *Echoes*, *Medusa's Kitchen*, *The Ophidian*, *Passages*, *Presa*, *Primal Urge*, *Rattlesnake Review*, *Ten Pages Press*, *WTF*, and *The Yolo Crow*. Hickerson grew up in New York City and New Jersey and had fond memories of reading her poetry in the bookstores and bars of San Francisco. She passed away in 2012, completing this manuscript shortly before her death.